THE UNREALITY OF TIME

& suddenly he awoke
in the midst of being awake

he can feel the brisk air brush against his skin
the calm sound of palm trees in the wind

he is aware of his presence
in the very essence

of everything else.

JIMMIE FLORA

THE UNREALITY OF TIME

NEW AND SELECTED POEMS
(2 0 0 6 - 2 0 1 8)

dedicated to malaan

PROLOGUE

PART I
Page 9

PART II
Page 35

PART III
Page 65

THE UNREALITY OF TIME
TABLE OF CONTENTS

PART I

INTRO

I have this fixation with the way memories fade
as each day passes
I find myself stuck like sand in hour glasses;

living in a time loop, unconscious of my behavior & actions.

repeating motions,
repeating mistakes

afraid to move forward, paralyzed by the negative thoughts
my mind creates.

I'm choosing to change
because change
is inevitable

& life
like everything else
is a series of moments unfolding
in this infinite illusion called time.

seasons never the same yet they rhyme.

when change disrupts the comfortability
of our day to day lives:

 accept it, stop resisting,
become resilient
& evolve

let go, let God

pave the way, ride the wave and exist at your own pace
in the Unreality of Time

POV

how do you view the truth?

is it a painful sting?
or just a slight pinch of a bee sting?

do you
take yourself out of your human skin
& see your life as a soul?

is the glass half empty or half full?

are your two eyes shut
& your third eye open?

from
what

is your perspective?

FREE BIRD

I'd love to be a bird
soaring between these buildings.

on edge,
feeling the untamed wind.

perched.

if only the sky was home,

if only I can escape this fear of dying alone.

vivid dreams of falling
never hitting the ground.

I want to live amongst the clouds

vanishing & reappearing into the Unknown.

I'd love to be a bird

free

 to fly away from it all.

OBLIVION

interdimensional

rhythm

we live in

the
seasons

we
flow

god given
you know?

spirit:

multiple colorful

vivid rays

glisten

I've found myself

being

lost

Vegas

I am just a soul

playing the role

of this human existence.

GALLIUM SPHINX MOTH

the sun silky warm

love metamorph like silk worm

PRECIPICE

& there I was
facing the infinite folds of
                time & space

the sound of distant ringing
like the soft humming of sirens

the taste of infinity on the tip of my tongue

so sweet

like nectarine.

LOST IN SPACE

how unsatisfying is the feeling
when I let my imagination roam
and to recall myself back to reality

& my mind does not come home..

A SHARP CIRCLE

I am fragile.

I am slivers of broken glass.

I am the metal between your lips
when I taste the liquor from the silver flask.

I am cut by shards
of my own broken promises

I am the bitter
sweet taste
of karma.

I caught a glimpse
of your mind in motion,

I might fall deep
in the pools of your eyes

like oceans.

MIDNIGHT IN A PERFECT WORLD

See
your mind wanders
like you are lost at
sea,

I am captivated by the way you are caught in deep thought
in front of me.

Gazing in those hazy dreams of future past,
You wish to stop the grain of sand from slipping in the hourglass.

At last,
how lovely to peer into a mind caught up in idea.

Can I interrupt you and watch you come back to this world?

May I corrupt you for a moment

for only a minute

Let me bring you back to the present time
to remind you how
it feels to be present
here & now.

35MM

we are moments
made like photographs

developed in a dark room
dimly lit

the slight gestures
of two silhouettes
captivate even the busiest of eyes

just a moment
captured

frozen in time

DATE NIGHT

"Have a taste of infinity. Come dine with me" He said.

Blush red.

I was allured by the sound of his voice & his choice of words.

 I made no hesitation to deny.

I replied with an eyebrow raised & a sparkle in my eye,

"You know I have a fascination with time
& the taste of infinity
just might satisfy
my appetite."

That night
I tried a slice of forever
& died.

He smiled & said,
"I'll pay for dessert."

With a touch of his cold fingers, he froze all my hurt and took my last breath.

I had a date with death

& oh!
he was such a gentleman.

SLEEP PARALYSIS

woke up in the middle of the night
vivid dreaming

I thought I saw a demon creeping on my chest.

I begged, "Please don't take my last breathe."

Praying to the holy ghost, "Help me get these hands up off my neck."

It's got my head.
It's got my legs.

I'm starting to lose control of my self.

My eyes to the back of my head.
My eyes to the back of my head.

I re awoke.
Pale white like ivory coke.

Cold sweating, heart racing.
Lightning bolt.

I couldn't scream.
I couldn't move.

3:33AM interlude

HYPNAGOGIA

imagine if
life is just a dream

slowly drifting in between

how I wish to wake up

BASQUIAT

If our existence is a work of art,
what portrait are you painting?

Are you coloring within the lines?

Do you let the ink bleed?

Do you get lost in someone else's design
of who they think you should be?

THE CHILD INSIDE

"Please don't forget me..."

says my innocence,
my inner child I grew to push away.
You still linger on to my restless thoughts
like you always want to play.

"Please don't forget..."

You say again, you are dying to be heard,
I'm too stubborn to even notice how--
you love to wander around my words.

"Please don't..."

 You tremble.

I'm choosing what isn't best..
This game we play isn't fun anymore,
close yours eyes and get some rest.

"Please..."

You're whithering away & far too weak.
I never allowed you to even speak.

"..."

It's eerie now but I question,
Why did I refuse to let you live?
It's my turn to whisper,
I hope you hears me...

"Please forgive..."

PHOENIX

the key

is to   be yourself

F R E E
Y O U R S E L F

25

Oh! Life is such a funny thing!
How humor helps a failing dream.
But memories blur--
& fade away.

I cannot control this disarray.

Long ago, I've always had--
these fascinations with time.

Fast forward to age twenty-five,
My mind whispers, "Who am I?"

I tend to wonder what could have been,
what should I've done,
& what if?

But one thing is for certain--
I still have more life to live.

The question still remains and I won't settle
for nothing less,

The only answer I am able to give--
is present through this text:

I am twenty-five,
I am still alive,
& for that, I am truly blessed.

BACK TO FOREVER

we forget that everything is temporary

we get worked up over issues that don't really matter

we regret our mistakes and we compare ourselves to each other

we fret about the frivolous things

we desensitize ourselves
because we're afraid of feelings

we forget about the importance of human connection

we're all plugged in yet
no connection

stuck in this dimension bound by the rules of time & space

we grow old
we die
and we return to that infinite place

the beauty of life
we forget to treasure

we are finite beings
trying to find our way

back to forever

SKY OF DIAMONDS

why
    is the meaning in
                Life

repeated
loops

of the infinite time

internet wires

mind is
shifting
      On plates

of
M U L T I
dimensional

skies.

UNSCATHED

my life, in and of itself is an ongoing master piece;
a spiritual collaborative effort between
me, myself & God.

& the muse to my soul is what I choose to be influenced by:
my loved ones, the positive people I've surrounded myself with

& the child inside me,
Unscathed

hear your truth

and speak it, too

no matter how much your voice
shakes & trembles

let your soul

spill
over

I still dream of moments
I will never get back

some nights
I want to
fade into the æther,

a gradient
of silent black

PART II

TWILIGHT

I used to be
able to see
that twinkle in your eye.

hypnotized by your starry gaze,

I remember those days
when you gave me shivers
down my spine.

why do you
look at me that way?

why don't you
look at me the same?

I look you in your eyes
& I see your soul,

those eyes are a dying star

a black hole.

ABYSS

there comes a time
in life, in love
two paths that intertwine untwist
and while we slowly unravel
 my heart travels to the abyss

to some degree, I lost myself
in you and you can't see

you're blind because I've lost you first
I've lost that look you give to me

I no longer get that warm embrace
at night when I can't sleep
I miss you more than what you know
because you think I'm full of deceit

I promise you I will do better

 of all my lies
this is true

knowing
our love is failing

catch me
I'm falling

I need
you

PARALLEL UNIVERSE

Unfortunately
 I've come to realize that out of all possible universes
we reside in the one where our paths no longer intertwine
like how ribbons seem to slowly unravel so delicately with time

I tremble with my thoughts of you
and this emptiness inside

Oh! How it pains to remember the pleasures
of what now only lingers in the mind

As our fate is spun on thread so thin
I apologize for all the hurt

I will always regret not showing you
how much love you truly deserve

& even in the misfortune of our realities
I only wish you to love once more

but never like the love we shared

because for a moment we were perfect

Never more.

LAST DANCE

Your aching fingers linger close
to an empty open palm

embrace my touch

I feel your breathe.

no sound
no lyrics

just song

MY HEART IS ON FIRE

I can't bear the wear and tear of a love lost

It feels like my heart is burning under a blistering fire
& I can't stop but admire

how beautifully lit my heart sits upon that flame

these past promises of love
meant to last a lifetime still linger
even after we've moved on.

I never thought that forever meant when we weren't together.

I can't wait until the day I can look into your eyes

& feel nothing.

2,920 DAYS OF YOU

I'm haunted by these thoughts of you everywhere I go,
This eerie silence echoes the broken pieces of my soul,

For I have died a thousand times by multiples of four,
Not once have I gone a day without wishing I wasn't scorned.

The remedy is so cynical, so simple yet I will not-
be a victim of my circumstance but I'm certain that I must not.

The ghosts of you just linger in the most obvious of places
like my heart,
my home,
the clothes I wear,
the music in my playlists.

My days are melancholic and my nights are filled with disarray,
I grieve for the death of us, I have to accept what was best for us.
I understand that it will never be the same.

So long, farewell, I know now that you are finally free.
I still mourn for the loss of us.

Rest In Peace.

ALL THE FUCKS I EVER GAVE

watch yourself wither into someone else
just give yourself away

no self preservation; whatsoever

I will never want you again

all the fucks I ever gave to you
you just gave to other men

I SHAVED MY HEAD BALD AFTER I WROTE THIS

the blood
rose red
drips down my nose
into the sink

my mind goes down the drain too

 I think?

I question whether life
withers like
everything else

a blush pink around my eyes

what a sad repeat of melancholy

life is only
a recycle of pain endured

I wish
my life
was another way

I wish
I knew a cure

SWEET NOTHINGS

my heart
now a hole

filled with
sweet nothings

FALLING STAR

my voice lingers in your after
thoughts

you admire me
from afar

my heart
engulfed in flames

but from your distance
a shooting star

INSIDIOUS

these past pains
get pushed aside

it never seems to go away

they latch onto my soul & create a home in the holes of my heart

like a stowaway.

the burden I bury will resurface nonetheless
infesting every inch & every corner of my head

simmering slowly in the back of my mind

the perfect poison
for a ponderous death

FORGET YOU

I purposely put myself in situations where I
would forget about you

like how I
got myself a tinder & right swiped every guy
just so I
could forget you

forget you

A SHALLOW POOL

I wish you would
look into my eyes
& seek my soul

see me whole

instead your eyes only wander

skin deep

AFTERGLOW

I remember when I felt this way with him

the way your thumb brushes my cheek & how you
caress my skin.

I'm kissing on you but I'm thinking about him

& I can't help it.

GHOST IN A SHELL

my soul
is aching

rotting in the remnants of who I once was

longing for something more
than
just

this..

SPECTRAL

you are now a blur
a thing of the past

a stranger in the room

a spectral in my
photographs

DAWN OF THE DEAD

in the early dawning of morning fog
lies a restless soul with unsettled thoughts.

I rot
laying here next to him with you still on my mind
haunting the empty hallways of my heart.

I cannot find peace
even with my head placed gently on soft clouds of
white pillows spread on bed sheets.

the blurring of last night's shame repeating
over and over again.

tossing & turning in a bed I should call my grave.

past mistakes
creep their way
back into my head.

back from the dead.

A LAVENDER ROSE

how numbing it is
to break your heart right from the start

you gave me your trust
& I played it like a harp

to pick the petals
off a bud of a rose still blooming

this is my own doing.

ROUND BROWN EYES

in an instant
I realized all the pain I caused you

a slight ringing in my ear
& this weight on my heart

your muffled screams
sharp

I can see the gloss glaze over those round brown eyes

your sad brown eyes

I can't forget all the ways I fucked with your heart

& even then
I looked you in those round brown eyes

and lied

RETICULATED PYTHON

this sorrow spirals around my neck
it slithers down my spine

creeping
crawling in my thoughts

it's rotting in my mind.

I am a shell just hollow

no soul,
no heart
just empty space

if dreaming is anything close to death
I'd sleep my days away

see
I am just as broken
but you will never know

I am getting better at smiling

so the pain will never show

some days I feel like nothing

nothing
at all

GRIME

& if it still hurts
I just redirect the pain

how I crumble
into nothing

feeling
every
single
grain

A WHITE ROSE

some people are exactly who they seem

no purpose imagining
a deeper meaning

nothing
but
a pretty face

a waste
of time & space

a rose, by any other name
would smell as sweet,

a blend of candles, perfume
& the deceased

A RED ROSE

how come you are careless with the rose I gave to
you?

you do not give it water

you let the sun dry up all its leaves

do you not see how delicate the flora is?

how beautiful each petal is?

how carefully trimmed are the thorns?

do you want this rose bud to blossom?

or

are you fine to just care

so little?

the rose,
my heart

the parallels.

you treat both
one in the same

FINE CHINA

wasn't it enough that he compared me to fine china

that I,
too fragile of a thing
must only be admired from the shelf

 he was afraid to feel my pain

a pain he knew too well

my fine china

QUIT PLAYING GAMES WITH MY HEART

can we not play the same game
the moon plays
with the ocean?

pulling
the
   tides

love
like
land
   slides.

E r o s
       i o n

A TIGER UNTAMED

I've come to discover my heart can break in new
ways.

this piercing pain,
all over again.

It's like a band aid ripping off an old wound too soon.

it seems to never end
because today
it feels like a tiger untamed,

shredding its sharp claws into my flesh,
its jaws sunk deep into my soft neck.

I still can feel my heart beat within my chest.

as I am mangled about,
tossed around like a chew toy.

my life flash before my eyes
& I experience all my pain
like it was a new joy.

there is never enough words to express
how my soul will come to rest.

I have died a thousand times yet this time
will be my death

SLIGHT PINCH OF A BEE STING

picking up the pieces of my soul up off the floor

the jagged edges prick my fingers

oh, so gently

REVERIE

these moments of missing you

are melting clocks
in hazy dreams

they simmer bright
in fading streams

of distant kisses
from shooting stars

the thought of you

a reverie

a faint
& fleeting

memory

ENIGMA

how can this be?

when life continues to wear your soul
 & break you down

you come back in one piece

PART III

A LILAC ROSE

he forgave himself
for past mistakes

he gave himself room to grow

he watered the roots & nurtured his soul

now
watch
him
bloom
 like a rose

DOLORES PARK

two hearts rendezvous
under the hazy hues of San Francisco

a blanket laid out on the basil green grass
quilted clouds of the purple green grass

shared
laughs

laying down their guards & insecurities like the
undressing of clothes

the very nature of who they are exposed

such an endearing birth
of infatuation

the blurring colors
of both their auras
chalk a soft pastel
 purple

 a moment
 of
 sincerity shared

full circle

19TH STREET / OAKLAND STATION

what I desire most
is to be the love song
strung up
on his lips

the touch of my caress
like a tune he won't forget

he,
a mystery
I am curious to solve

I wonder
whether
he
thinks the same

of me

THE UNREALITY OF TIME

I
   drift
       away
          s l o w l y
               in the depths of your eyes

   you make me
          forget
  where   I am.

our souls

make love

        in the middle

             of where we stand

like a solved riddle

if

 perchance

MALAAN

Oh, how the light fell
beautifully
 from his smile
 to his eyes

the soft glow
between his brow
traces
    down
   to
his
  inner thighs

Sulking up the sun rays

EVENT HORIZON

lost between
the lines which separate

me   from   you.

a blending
& blurring
of our bodies bring

soft
warm waves
of red

like the hues
of the sunset

in the heat
between dusk

overlooking
a sand dune,

the sweet
subtle colors

of a late night
mid june

.WAV

the sound of your voice
lingers in my mind
like a tune I can't quite remember

souls that sung
 once
in past life times

I swear
you feel
so familiar

NINA SIMONE & MARY JANE

mid summer
mornings

& the scent
of fresh flora.

sweet hues
of indigo

he adorns
the soft colors

of
my
aura

BRILLIANCE

love
like
light

playfully teasing through the striped lines
between the blinds of an open window

the warm glow finesses every groove
& smooth rhythm of your skin

4TH OF JULY

laying down
on soft clouds
of loud
ganja green

I woke up
in a blue dream

eyes
red
white stars
and
him
in blue jeans

LONG EXPOSURE

you & I

lock eyes

your gaze

penetrates mine

we kiss

we stop time

long exposure

SILENT NIGHT

I enjoy the moments when
we don't speak a word

& we simply gaze deep
into each other's eyes

I hope you find the home you've
been longing for

in the comfort of mine

I forget where I am
& I lose track
of time

because your smile
 a spell

and I'm hypnotized.

A WILD ROSE

I'm situated between
the gentle touch
of your skin
pressed against my own,

my heart a wild rose
& you

ready to trim the thorns.

I'll never let you go.

you've made a home inside my soul.

from the words you carefully chose
to the soft subtle kisses whispered in my ear

in the silence of the night
when only I can hear

"I love you."

A LOVE LIKE INFINITY

I want to take my time with you
spend infinity appreciating every ounce of you and your worth.
not only on this earth but throughout the vastness of the universe

beginning and end

no beginning
no end

love
all over again

transcending
dimensions of time & space
take me to our sacred place
where we can love freely

two souls
new souls
two hearts
new ages

rediscovering each other like
the hundreds of lifetimes before

yet,
in this very moment
we lock eyes
like we just
first met

lets explore.

CPSIA information can be obtained
at www.ICGtesting.com
Printed in the USA
LVHW050430250220
648118LV00006B/250

9 780464 723295